RYA Coacl

CW00821848

Former RYA Coach.

Edited by Mike Hart
RYA Coaching Development Officer
Foreword by Chris Gowers
Olympic Laser Coach

© RYA 2009
First Published 2009
Reprinted 2010
Reprinted 2011
The Royal Yachting Association
RYA House, Ensign Way, Hamble
Southampton SO31 4YA
Tel: 0844 556 9555
Fax: 0844 556 9516
Email: publications@rya.org.uk
Web: www.rya.org.uk

A CIP record of this book is available from the British Library

Note: While all reasonable care has been taken in the preparation
of this book, the publisher takes no responsibility for the use of the
methods or products or contracts described in the book.

Telephone 0844 556 9555 for a free copy of our
Publications Catalogue.

Cover Design: Creativebyte
Photographs: RYA, Richard Langdon / Ocean Images
Illustrations: RYA
Typeset: Creativebyte
Printing: World Print

*Totally Chlorine
Free*   *Sustainable
Forests*

Contents

Great coaches inspire enthusiasm even with mundane tasks.

Introduction

When 759 Olympians generated 3178 success factors, the 5 highest factors were:-	1. Family and friends	58%
	2. Dedication and persistence	52%
	3. Coaches	49%
	4. Love of the sport	27%
	5. Training programmes	22%

This book is designed to help the coach provide the learning environment. In order to collect the content for this book I have quizzed a range of experienced coaches, sought out coaching experts and applied my own experience to help create some shape for the coaching routines we all take for granted. This is not a template for great coaching, only people can do that, but it will hopefully provide some of the concepts and systems that great coaches use.

Coaching is all about helping people to develop and change. In short it is about creating a learning environment, while supporting and challenging the sailor and adding shape to the process.

It is not about telling sailors what to do. The more you tell the less they develop the ability to decide for themselves. It may be easy in the short term but it doesn't create independent or creative athletes in the long term.

The last point about this book is that it is open to change and your opinion and ideas about what makes good coaching should help us amend later additions to create a workable and practical tool for all racing coaches.

Alan Olive
RYA Coaching Development Manager
(1999 – 2008)

Phil Slater
Cathy Foster
Mark Littlejohn
Chris Gowers
Jim Saltonstall
John Derbyshire
David Howlett
Rod Davis
Jez Fanstone
- The list of coaches who worked
with Gold medallist Ben Ainslie

Whose list will you be on?

The 5 Essentials for Coaching

Before I start talking about coaching I want to emphasise 2 things:

- Firstly, the importance of self practice. There are some sailors that don't go sailing without a coach and I think that prevents the ability to make good tactical decisions. Many of our best sailors spend a large amount of time training by themselves.
- Secondly, learning how to coach will improve your sailing because you will have a better understanding of how to learn.

1. Coaching qualifications

Qualifications	Course aims	Course length	Education and Development (CPD)
Racing Coach (Level 2)	To provide the basic skills to safely run a brief, on the water exercise and debrief	1 weekend Apply online	Top Mark, Clubs Conference, Junior CPD and the RYA Dingy Sailing Show
Junior and Youth Racing Coach Course	An in depth version of the Level 2 Racing Coach run for top sailors or ex-youth/ Junior Squad sailors	5 days Includes first aid and powerboat level 2. Apply to RYA Coaching Development Team	Top Mark, Clubs Conference, Junior CPD and the RYA Dingy Sailing Show
Racing Coach (Level 3)	To provide a thorough understanding of how people learn and how to coach. Core subjects and skills such as creating sailor programmes, rules, managing squads and sail and rig and foils	2 weekends , task book, assessment and mentoring (10 months) Apply online	RYA Coaching Professional Development (2-6 days per year)
National Racing Coach (Level 4)	Individual programme based around the World Class Coaching Development Programme	By appointment only. Apply to RYA Coaching Development Team	World Class Coaching Professional Development (4-8 days per year)

2. Finding a good coach

The best sailors don't always make the best coaches and yet the majority of sailors select coaches based on the coaches sailing ability. Ironically your best coach in the world is actually you. Coaches can give you a good head start in your training but only you can apply those skills and knowledge while racing. Here are some ideas to help you find the right coach to help you develop your racing skills.

- Identify what is going to make a difference to your sailing e.g. starts, tactics, boat handling.
- Pick a coach that has expertise in the area and your class.

The best people to advise you on whom to pick are:
- Your own coach.
- The Youth Racing Manager.
- Your HPM.
- The Coaching Development Team.

If you have a squad coach, **always** make sure that you tell them that you are also working with another coach, so they can both compliment what they are each saying. Different opinions are good but they shouldn't conflict.

3. What makes a good coach?

Good coaches are those that allow you to develop all of your racing skills.
They should:
- Be a good listener
- Be organised and safe
- Be there for you to talk to and trust
- Avoid talking too much e.g. lectures
- Try to understand how you learn
- Run fun sessions
- Have a good knowledge of the sport and your class

Word of advice: Many coaches feel that they have to tell you as much as possible and hope that some of it will make a difference. The best coaches talk less but make sure that what they do say is very important for you. Some of the best learning goes on in the boat, not the classroom.

4. The essential check list for being coached:

- Does the coach have RYA racing coaching qualifications? (All coaches should carry a coaching ID card.)
- Do they have a current first aid qualification?
- Do they have a RYA powerboat qualification?
- Do they have coaching insurance? Are they working at the club with the club's permission, or is it an RYA run event?
- If the coach boat is borrowed, do they have written permission to use it?

5. Coaching Professional Development (CPD)

All coaches need to develop their own skills and the RYA run a range of events for different levels of coaches. These events involve sailing and coaching experts who provide the best tools and ideas on how to coach more effectively.

Event	Who is it for	How to attend?
Clubs Conference : • Annually • 1 day • Run locally • Normally December	Coaches working in clubs	Via your HPM
Top Mark • Run for specific classes • March-July	Coaches working in classes	RYA Coaching Development Team
Junior CPD • First weekend in September	Junior and Youth squad coaches	RYA Coaching Development Team
World Class CPD • 4 – 8 days a year • February and October	National and Olympic Coaches	RYA Coaching Development Team

RYA Coaching Ethics

Coaching sailing develops individuals by improving their sporting performance.

This is achieved by:

- Identifying and meeting the needs of individuals.
- Improving performance through a programme of safe, guided practice, measured performance and competition.
- Creating an environment in which individuals are motivated to maintain participation and improve performance.

Coaches should apply these principles of good practice:

- All RYA Coaches working with sailors under the age of 18 must read and understand the RYA Child Protection Policy.
- Coaches must respect the rights, dignity and worth of every person and treat everyone equally.
- Coaches must place the well-being and safety of the sailor above performance.
- Coaches must develop appropriate working relationships based on mutual trust and respect.
- Coaches must not abuse their position of authority for personal gain.
- Coaches must encourage sailors to accept responsibility for their own behaviour and performance.
- Coaches should hold the relevant RYA qualifications.
- Coaches must ensure activities are appropriate for the age, maturity, experience and ability of the individual.
- Coaches should, at the outset, clarify with sailors (and where appropriate with their parents) exactly what is expected of them and what they are entitled to expect from their coach. A contract may be appropriate.
- Coaches should co-operate with other specialists (eg. other coaches, officials, sports scientists, doctors, physiotherapists) in the best interests of the sailor.
- Coaches should always promote the positive aspects of their sport (eg. fair play) and never condone rule violations or the use of prohibited substances.
- Coaches must consistently display high standards of behaviour and appearance.

SECTION 1: Coaching Principles

Coaching: Helping to change others

A successful coach loves what they do, and their job is their passion. Coaching is not easy, nor does it always receive recognition of the effort it takes to perform. It involves developing a sailor physically and emotionally, technically and socially. A coach needs knowledge, skills, experience, and a strong coaching philosophy.

It is also vital sailors become their own coach as well as rely on you. The coaches time is always at a premium and they have to prioritise specific issues. Sailors also have to take responsibility for their own learning and training.

The 5 essentials of sailing

- Course made good
- Balance
- Trim
- Sail setting
- Centreboard

The 8 essentials of coaching

Coaching the sailor to be their own coach!
- Plan
- Prime
- Do
- Feedback
- Review
- Safety
- Enjoyment
- Know your sailors

Plan - Prime - Do - Feedback - Review

Create programme (Plan)
- Identify race area and skill

Brief (Prime)
- Goal setting
  (Technique training = Process and Skill)
- Explain the exercises

On the water (DO)
- Optimising the learning environment

Feedback
- As close to the event/action as possible

Debrief (Review)
- Summarise feedback, plan future training

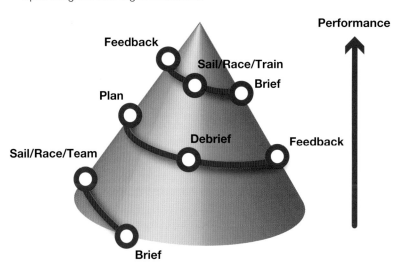

The 10 key racing elements

1. Learning how to learn and develop
2. Self preparation (mental and physical)
3. Boat preparation
4. Boat handling
5. Boat tuning and speed
6. Strategy and Met (the quickest route around the course)
7. Tactics (the route with other boats)
8. Starting
9. Teamwork
10. Racing rules

How to be a great coach

- Get to know your sailors, how to inspire them, how to talk to them, how they learn etc.
- Coach the sailor to be their own coach. Involve your sailors in the process.
- Strive to be the best - what can you do better?
- Selfless not selfish.
- Fascination for the process. Immerse yourself in sport and coaching.
- Actively learn yourself: remain competitive in your sailing, try to learn new subjects and new sports.
- Study the best.
- Try to make your sport and coaching scientific: research, experiment, measure changes, analyse, record. But never lose touch with the artistic side of the process.
- Challenge your sailors and yourself.
- Master the process of communication - a 2 way process!.
- Be creative - collect great ideas when you see them.
- Manage your team by inspiring self learning and self discipline.
- Optimise learning in everything you do - accept quality feedback from as many sources as possible.
- Plan, prime, do, feedback, review.
- Safety first.
- Success is not always about winning!

SECTION 2: Coaching Fundamentals

2.1   Optimising learning in others

Coaches teach best when they:
- Include variety and fun in everything.
- Create training in bite sized chunks.
- Provide focus to all training and racing - whenever possible directed by the sailor.
- Provide feedback (verbal, video, speed, outcome, etc.).
- Provide best practice by the use of top sailors or video clips. Imitation is a powerful learning process.
- Coach with a variety of styles and formats, e.g. verbal, articles, diagrams, videos, doing, etc. Make sure you relate this to your sailors' learning styles (Honey and Mumford).
- Avoid talking too much.
- Minimise debriefs, focus on the 'nuggets'. People rarely take away more than 3 things per session/weekend, so make sure they are important ones.

Sailors learn best when:
- They understand how they learn effectively (Honey and Mumford). Get the sailors to recognise how they learn best.
- They feel confident to express their thoughts and ideas.
- They are allowed to experiment and play.
- The lessons relate to things they already know.
- They are allowed to make mistakes and to experience success (both are needed to learn).

2.2 Developing skill and technique

Technique: *"The physical movements that make up a manoeuvre."*

Skill: *"The ability to perform a technique appropriate to the conditions, at will and consistently while under pressure. Right skill, right time, right place!"*

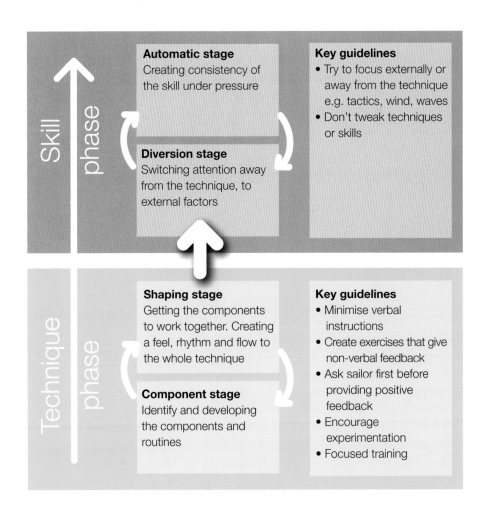

2.3 Planning and preparation

"Failing to plan is planning to fail". Abraham Lincoln

Plan, prepare, do, review:

Goal/Objective

Role/job   Resources   Barriers

Plan

Delegate/communicate   Feedback/review

Manage/Coach

Perform

Try to include the sailor in the planning process as much as possible.

2.3   Planning and preparation

Has to come from the sailor:
- The key to motivation (and communication) is to make it important and specific to the individual.
- People do things for their reasons, not yours.
- Success and failure are both significant for developing motivation.
- Confidence is the balance between perceived ability and the challenge faced.
- Understand how to reward your sailor. Praise, attention, etc.

Coaching behaviours:
- Only reward the behaviours you want.
- Publicly praise, privately admonish.
- Reduce rewards as skill develops.
- Develop your relationship with your sailors so that you understand how and what to say to reward and challenge them and when to do it.
- Know when to reward winning and effort.
- Everyone has the ability to become talented.

2.5   Communication

Very little of what people take in is related to what we actually say. Body language, eye to eye contact, tone of voice, the clothes you wear as well as how you speak have a powerful influence on the message received.

* 55% - body language
* 38% - tone of voice
* 7% - what you say

Communication is a multi-sensory process:

Visual: pictures, diagrams, video.
Audio: spoken word.
Reading: books, e-mails, text, etc.
Kinaesthetic: doing, feeling, dry drills, etc.

Golden rule: The Big 3!
Keep all briefs, feedback and debriefs focused on no more than 3 things.

Top Tips:
* Communication is a 2 way process.
* KISS – keep briefs and debriefs focused on a maximum of three things.
* Don't rely on just words to coach. Most people get more from diagrams, pictures, video, demonstrations, written notes and doing.
* Use language that can be understood by the sailor.
* Use questions to check what has been understood and to involve the sailors in the learning process.
* Actively listen, don't just hear.

2.6   Leadership

- Lead by example and exhibit the standards and behaviours you expect from your sailors.
- Enthusiasm inspires.
- Know yourself and seek to improve.
- Accept feedback.
- Support and respect your sailors (see code of conduct).
- Give your sailors responsibility to run their own development as well as the teams (ownership).
- Communicate, communicate and communicate!
- Plan and prepare thoroughly. The bedrock of an effective leader.
- Be decisive when you need to but involve the team in decisions whenever time permits.
- Honesty and integrity are the currency of good coaching.

Leading by example has a powerful influence on your sailors, but remember that the values you coach need to extend to your personal sailing as well.

2.7   Knowledge of the sport

- Fascination for the process.
- Understand when to make sailing and coaching a science and when to make it an art.
- All coaches need to compete on a regular basis.
- If you want to know the answer, ask a real expert.
- Surround yourself with experts.
- Leave no stone unturned.
- Avoid pet theories.
- Work with other coaches as often as possible and at as many levels as possible.

It is important for coaches to compete on a regular basis to understand the challenges and skills needed to race.

2.8   Safety

As a coach you have a duty of care: *"You must take reasonable care to avoid acts or omissions which you could reasonably foresee which would be likely to injure your sailor."*

- The risk of getting it wrong is death.
- Never underestimate the potential for something to go wrong.
- Being safe should not remove the fun and excitement of our sport.
- Disregarding safety issues and procedures does not make it cool or fun.
- Identify the hazards and dangers and try to minimise the risks.
- Every emergency is different so you need to equip yourself with as many skills as possible. This can only be achieved by practice.
- Preparation and training.
- Effective communication is essential when dealing with emergencies.
- Know your sailors, needs, abilities and medical issues.

See Section 3.9 (page 38) "Coaching Checklists" for further information.

2.9　Fun and health

Variety is an essential ingredient:
- Games are great for inspiring fun and developing skills.
- Coaches need to be enjoying themselves to inspire fun in their sailors. Make sure your programme inspires you as well as your sailors.
- Racing is fun but only when you're doing well. Effective coaching allows everyone to win at some time.
- Reward effort as well as performance if you want to inspire hard working sailors.
- Let sailors choose the fun games whenever you can.

"You really are what you put into your body. You can't run on fumes. You don't put a lousy gasoline in a top-quality car." - Martina Navratilova

- Fad diets rarely work. Regular exercise and gradual changes are much better to create permanent changes.
- Parental education is a significant factor for developing healthy eating.
- Dehydration is a concentration killer.
- Sailing relies on a multitude of core skills and mental awareness. Young sailors need to be encouraged to participate in a range of sports, especially between the ages of 8-12.

Fun is the most important factor that will attract people to the sport and keep them sailing.

2.10   Winning

- When you're winning, don't change what you're doing.
- Don't change things for regattas without testing them out in training.
- Avoid the corner.
- Winners love to win; it's all they care about.
- 98% Perspiration, 2% Inspiration.
- Luck favours the well prepared.
- An idiot is someone who continues to do the same things and expects a different result.

If you follow this basic cycle you put yourself in a position to win but there are some other parameters rugby world cup coach Yehuda Shinar says you have to consider:

- Stick to the basics.
- Use proven methods – if it isn't broke don't fix it.
- Avoid wrong methods – if it didn't work before it still won't work. Yehuda calls these "corners" - very apt for sailing! So winning is simple - avoid the "corners" or losing methods. Don't fall in love with your own pet theories.
- Self control – control feelings of stress, anxiety and frustration.
- Thoroughness.
- Decisiveness.
- Time management.
- Handling one-on-one situations – when a competitor puts pressure on, respond by putting pressure on them, but more. Harm their self confidence.

2.11 Developing the sailor-coach relationship

Key words:
Honest, open, fair, consistent, positive, supportive, challenging.

Your role as a coach is to facilitate the sailor learning. You can't control this process without the sailor's involvement, approval and 'buy in'.

- Sailor and coach should create the team culture, standards, rewards and forfeits.
- Identify the goals and programme for the sailor.
- Identify how the sailor learns best.
- Identify how the coach can support and encourage that learning.
- Identify how to maintain the standards being set. What are the rules and how are they enforced?
- Create confidential and open systems to allow the sailor to provide feedback to the coach.
- Create an open system of communication.
- Be proactive about accepting feedback.
- Treat every one equally (as much as possible) and try to spread your time equally among the squad. Try to avoid developing favourites.

Trust and respect are at the heart of any good working relationship.

SECTION 3: Coaching Checklists

3.1   Running a race training weekend

Preparation:

- Book equipment and resources: RIB, classroom, radios, etc.
- Talk to the club (especially 2 weeks before) and identify who will be your rep for the weekend (get their mobile number). Talk them through the programme step by step.
- Create a focus to the weekend e.g. starts, tactics, boat handling.
- E-mail the sailors the details of the weekend (priming). See Remote Coaching Checklists (Section 3.6). Ask them what they want to focus on and set them some homework to get them thinking about the weekend.
- Contact the assistants/team, defining the jobs for the weekend (make sure you phone as well).
- Prepare lessons plans (include bad weather alternative).

Two days before:

- Check your coaching equipment.
- Check the weather forecast.
- Rehearse your lesson plans.

On the day (see Event Safety Management checklist):

Meet the club rep -

- Confirm classroom and facilities with the club rep.
- Rib radios.
- Club safety brief.
- Club hazards: Read the club operating manual or at least review the key operating information about the club.
- Where are the sailors parking/rigging, launching etc.

Briefings:
Meet and brief the assistants (coaching team) -
* Confirm their roles and tasks.
* Conduct brief risk assessment with assistants and plan for the most likely problems (see Safety checklists, Section 3.9).

Meet and greet sailors and parents (if appropriate) -
* Register all sailors attending.
* Medical requirements/issues.
* Parental consent forms.
* Payments etc.

Brief the sailors and parents on the weekend programme -
* Housekeeping.
* The focus for the weekend.
* General hazards and routines associated with club.

Break into coaching groups for group briefs.

On the water:
* Register all sailors going afloat.
* Communications with each coaching group.
* Keep an eye on conditions and all groups.
* Have fun.
* Food, fluids, sunscreen, toilet, etc.
* Sometimes shorter sessions maintain concentration than one long session.

After sailing:
* Ensure everyone is accounted for.
* Arrange time, place and resources for debrief.

Debrief:
* Review lessons learnt.
* Involve the sailors – "Ask, Discuss, Solve".
* Create action plans for future training.
* View video footage.
* Debrief parents if needed (there are the ones that can help support the lessons learnt).

Post weekend report
Provide written report/feedback to sailors with their action plan.

Feedback

Don't forget to get feedback from sailors and from parents/assistants you think will be constructive and informed. This can be done anonymously but is always best achieved by creating an environment where you are keen to hear their thoughts so that you can develop your coaching skills. Questionnaires can be very useful sources as long as you keep them short and specific.

Setting the standards:

- No drinking, no sex.
- Dampen party expectations.
- Get involved with all activities: help with equipment.
- Kids take the lead from leaders: remain calm and upbeat.
- Vagueness is contagious.
- Maximum manageable group size: 5 boats, 8-10 sailors.
- Read RYA safety guidelines.
- With kids, what are you doing for non-squad members of the team? Make sure they know before getting afloat (include their parents in that cycle).

Event management:

List of sailors' names available. Emergency details, allocate rooms, curfew, alcohol, breakfast etc.

- Sailor code of conduct established, on and off water.
- Health declaration/disclaimer, signed and problems noted.
- Medication to hand for those with specific needs such as diabetes, allergies, asthma, etc.
- Venue sailing instructions - signing on/off, tag system, warning flags, etc.

Boat safety and ratios:

- Sufficient safety boats available for session, conditions and sailors.
- Sufficient coaches to sailors.
- Safety boat club requirements - two people in the boat? Driver has a minimum of RYA Powerboat Level 2?
- Boat safety kit, first aid kit, kill cord and fuel checked before launching.
- Boat to boat, boat to shore signals established. Are radios available?
- All sailors accounted for at beginning and end of session.

Accident procedures:
- Note location of club first aid point, and telephone availability.
- Is club appointed first aid officer available on day? If not, who is responsible?
- Hospital location known.
- Accident book to be filled in. Full details should be recorded and club informed.

Pre-launch briefing:
- Sailing area established, and zones if required.
- Sufficient drinks/food carried for duration of session?
- Launch, landing and safe kit storage established.
- Buoyancy requirements observed.
- Sailors recall/regroup signals established.
- Sailors aware of session duration.
- Inform coach if leaving session.

3.2　Briefings – Creating the learning environment

When choosing an exercise the coach must decide what skill is being developed and how that exercise will provide feedback to the sailor.

The aims of the brief are to:

1. Create the focus/goals/objectives for the session.
2. Get the sailors in the right frame of mind to learn (priming).
3. Make sure everyone understands what the plan is.

Preparation

The area you chose to brief in will set the flavour for the rest of the exercise:

- Inside or outside?
- Can all the sailors see the board/visual aids?
- Can they all hear you?
- Sitting or standing? Enough chairs?
- Have you minimised distractions?
- Do you need to shape the classroom?

Equipment:
- White/black board.
- Notes and session plan.
- Pens and wiper.
- Video clips.
- Lesson plan.

Content:
- Introduce the subject.
- Brain storm the subject.
- Pick one key point you want to focus on and explain what they need to do. Establish the key coaching points for developing the technique or skill.
- Create a focus for the training (max 3 areas to be covered). Feedback should only cover these areas.
- Explain what the feedback will be.
- Use video or demonstration, dry drill to rehearse the skill (try to minimise the talking and focus on the coaching key points).
- Explain the exercise (draw the course on the board).
- Safety issues - what to do if……
- Hand and sound signals.
- Discuss any routines you want to establish e.g. always pass the coach boat after you finish the exercise/race. Don't launch until …. etc.
- Describe the sailing area and define the boundaries.
- Weather forecast.
- Questions to test understanding.
- Summarise and confirm goals for each boat and sailor.

Delivery:
- Coaching delivery and styles need to include:
  - **Visual**
  - **Audio**
  - **Reading**
  - **Kinaesthetic (doing)**
- Try to use as many senses as possible during the brief.
- Enthusiastic body language, tone of voice and eye to eye contact.
- Keep it short and simple (KISS) - remember the real learning is on the water.
- Draw the course on the board.
- Make sure you take notes of the goals for each sailor.
- Avoid jargon and check people understand the language you are using (never assume they do).
- Use first names if possible.
- When brain storming, always write down what they say.
- Try to involve everyone in the briefing.
- Questions Use questions throughout to engage with the sailors and to test what they have learnt. Open and closed.
  - **Pose,**
  - **Pause,**
  - **Pounce!**

3.3   On the water exercises

When choosing an exercise the coach must decide what skill is being developed and how that exercise will provide feedback to the sailor.

A good exercise should:

- Keep the sailors busy.
- Simulate real situations in the race course.
- Allow time for the sailor to practise by themselves.
- Be appropriate for the conditions and skill level of the sailors.
- Provide feedback (see notes on Feedback).

Tips for getting the exercise to run smoothly:

- Keep the sailors busy (pre-exercise activity).
- Brief signals and safety.
- Always think through a risk assessment - what if someone gets injured?
- Be flexible.
- Prepare coaching kit.
- Launching and recovery in pairs.
- Create regular routines to get sailors to circle the coach boat after each exercise.
- Allow time to be able to provide feedback to the sailors.
- Take notes for debrief (some people prefer a Dictaphone).
- Use assistants when ever possible, especially when videoing.
- Try to avoid chasing boats; many exercises are best run by remaining in one position.

Communication afloat:

- Be seen, be heard, test they can hear you.
- Don't talk through sails.
- Do you need to turn the engine off?
- Make sure you face towards them.
- Hove to or alongside before you try talking.
- Get the sailors to circle the rib.
- Have a set routine.
- Use first names.
- Eye to eye contact (no sun glasses if possible).
- Consistent, enthusiastic body language.

3.4   Feedback - the essential factor for learning

Feedback = Information on the sailor's performance

When choosing an exercise the coach must decide what skill is being developed and how that exercise will provide feedback to the sailor.

Feedback like any information, can be absorbed by any sense, but is most powerful when it is linked to feelings, thoughts and observations that the sailor notices themselves.

Allowing the sailor to learn by themselves is a powerful part of good coaching. Not only does it create a longer lasting memory but it also enhances their ability to make decisions which in turn is linked to confidence. A good coach helps the sailor develop their own powers of analysis by prompting and priming (done by remote coaching and briefs).

Feedback types:
Can include visual, audio, reading and feelings
- Coaches observations.
- Video footage.
- Still photos.
- Timings e.g. hoists, drops, gybes.
- Scores out of 10 for a manoeuvre.
- Time to get up to speed after a manoeuvre.
- Speed.
- Internal feelings and thoughts.
- Results.
- One boat sailing faster than another (2 boat tuning, tacking practise, etc).

Key principles:
- The more measurable the feedback the more objective it will be.
- The most powerful learning process is for a sailor to observe themselves or an expert either by a demonstration or video clip.
- Feedback has maximum effect when it is delivered as close to the manoeuvre, event or behaviour as possible. For example when one boat pulls ahead when sailing waves, showing a video clip on the water, rather than waiting for the classroom (if weather permits).

Verbal feedback - telling is not coaching!

Most coaches believe that feedback can only be delivered by talking. The reality is that talking can actually reduce the learning for the sailor. Coaches need to use a variety of sources of feedback. The RYA traffic light is the best way to deliver verbal feedback.

The RYA Traffic Light
Shaping the verbal feedback

Ask — Question - e.g. What did you notice? When, where and how much? Get them to be specific

Discuss — Your comments on their judgements and performance. Positive feedback!

Solve — Information on how to improve (Action plan/goal setting/focus)

Video footage, like any feedback, is a powerful tool for the coach but it needs to be focused to be effective (excuse the pun).

3.5   The debrief

The aim of the debrief is to:

- Review individual feedback from on the water.
- Summarise the lessons learnt from the session.
- Create an action plan to develop technique or skill in the future.
- Generate feedback for the coach.

Content:

- Revisit the aims of the session.
- Edit video by pre-viewing and noting sections that are useful. Avoid the 'home movie' syndrome.
- KISS.
- Feedback to include visual, audio, reading, kinaesthetic (doing and feeling) elements.
- Use the sailors experience to identify the key learning points of the exercise.
- Create an action plan for what they need to work on.
- Identify exercises and training ideas that will allow them to work on those techniques/skills by themselves.

Delivery:

- Keep to the specific goals determined in the brief. If sailors want more then talk to them afterwards. Feedback should only cover these areas.
- Ask their opinion first before providing information.
- Involve the sailors with open questions to bring out the key points of the session?
- Give individual and specific feedback on the sailors' performance.
- Use coaching notes when discussing feedback. Memory will rarely be good enough.
- Coaching delivery and styles need to include:
  - o **Visual**
  - o **Audio**
  - o **Reading**
  - o **Kinaesthetic (doing)**
- Enthusiastic body language, tone of voice and eye to eye contact.
- Keep it short and simple (KISS) - remember the real learning is on the water.
- Use first names if possible.
- When brain storming, always write down what **they** say.
- Try to involve everyone in the debriefing.
- **Questions** Use questions throughout to engage with the sailors and to test what they have learnt. Open and closed. **Pose, Pause, Pounce!**
- Make sure you take notes of the sailor's feedback and action plans.

3.6 Remote coaching

Prime-do-review

"The learning that takes place outside formal training"

A large part of the coach's job is to coach the sailor to be able to train by themselves. If we are training our sailors to be their own coach we need to give them the opportunities to practise.

The key issues in remote coaching are to get sailors to think about and practise sailing techniques and ideas away from the coach.

Remote coaching relies on being able to communicate with your sailors and the motivation of the sailor to actually get involved in the process. Both of which can be controlled by the coach.

Pre-training coaching ideas

Select the theme of focus for the training:

- Weekend's programme. Make the training relate to real racing scenarios and events that the sailors are planning to attend.
- Get the sailors to set goals and objectives for what they are trying to develop. Make sure that they identify what level they are at as well.
- Still Pictures: Send a picture and ask them a question that gets them thinking. e.g. what tactics would you be using if you were defending the lead in this picture? What do you notice about the shapes of spinnakers in this picture?
- Quizzes and games.
- Pre-reading. There are some great websites and articles on the internet (see the resources section). Get your sailors looking at these. You can always scan in pages and send them if you have some good books.
- Video clips. If you have the software, send a clip and ask them to analyse it. Again, keep it focused on what you're intending to cover during the weekend. Video clips could include best practice from an expert sailor. This might be more powerful than sending them a clip of themselves.
- Random instructions. Adam Bowers is renowned for including tasks in his sailor's homework to test whether they read his notes, e.g. everyone to wear a hat in the briefings!
- Creating your own web page or blog.
- Create your own pod cast if you have an MP3 player.

Ideas for training weekends:

If you want to get sailors to train by themselves you need to coach them how to do it.
- Incorporate exercises that can be used by the sailors in their own training. It is important to ensure that the sailor understands the feedback (i.e. information on how they are improving) for each exercise.
- Make sure that they know how to analyse their own performance by themselves. Make sure your coaching styles become less instructive and more informative. This may require you to let them make mistakes.
- Give them examples and ideas of how to train without buoys, start lines, etc.
- Set homework during the debriefs and make sure you summarise this in the post weekend notes. Unless you are testing their note taking skills.
- Try to create stills, pictures or video clips that will help the sailor remember the key learning points and refer to them during their own training.
- Always end the training with a summary and encourage sailors to debrief in teams and take notes.
- Encourage sailors to keep diaries from their training to record the lessons they learnt.

Post weekend work:
- Make sure that the report gets sent as soon as possible.
- Using a mobile text can be useful to get sailors thinking about analysing the weekend while in the car. This may need some prompting by the parents.
- Teach the parents how to **facilitate a positive** debriefing session with their kids.
- Always send a report with the key lessons learnt from the weekend. It doesn't have to be complex. Try to include real examples, pictures, clips and diagrams if needed.
- Take turns for the sailors to write up the weekend about what they enjoyed and learnt.
- Posting results, pictures and video clips. You may need to include this to the parents who can help ensure the homework gets done (especially if they are sailors themselves).
- Get them to sail in other classes and make sure they keep the fun element within their sailing.

3.7   Equipment and kit

Essential personal kit:
- Serrated knife or heavy duty scissors.
- Whistle.
- Buoyancy aid or lifejacket of the required size and standard.
- Mobile phone.
- Medical info summary.
- Emergency contact summary.
- First aid kit including survival blanket (not space blanket).
- Wet notes or dictaphone.

Additional personal Kit:
- VHF Radio.
- Compass.
- Wind indicator.
- Tide sticks.
- Anemometer.
- Burgee.
- Spare clothing/food/drink.
- Tool kit/repair kit.
- Wire cutters.
- Duck tape.
- Waterproof container for labelled inhalers.

Coach boat kit:
- Spare kill cord.
- Paddles or oars.
- Bucket or bailer.
- Fire extinguisher.
- Bridle secured to towing eyes.
- Towline.
- Spare starting cord and minimal tool kit.
- Chain and warp as appropriate.
- Bow anchor sufficient for safety boat and any towed craft.
- Distress flares - 2 orange smoke and 2 pinpoint red, or 2 day/night flares.

3.8   Planning and preparation

"Failing to plan is planning to fail".

(Try to include the sailor in as much of this as possible)

See illustration page 14
1.   Identify key events and define
     the annual goal (Outcome goal).
2.   Identify all other events in the programme, e.g. training
     and competition.
3.   Assess the skills needed and the priorities for training (select list from sailor
     profile and the 10 Racing Elements). Don't bite off too much - (KISS). This can
     include a tick list for a range different conditions and specific skills that sailors
     need to practise in. This allows you to be flexible for the conditions experienced
     during training.
4.   Divide the programme into phases:
     a.   Foundation (Training- fitness, boat prep, mental prep, boat handling,
          boat speed and basic racing skills).
     b.   Pre-competition (Race simulation- tactics, race routines, mental skills,
          applying pressure).
     c.   Competition (Race craft- tactics and strategy).
     d.   Rest/regeneration (time off from racing, having fun, maintaining health
          and fitness).
5.   Plan for the development of technique/skill from training to competition.
6.   Identify the priorities, goals for each phase of the programme.
7.   Establish the general goals and priorities for each training weekend (specific
     and measurable).
8.   Establish the general goals and priorities for each competition.
9.   Create a programme for each event - a generic focus.
10. Send out pre-event 'homework' (priming).
11. Check the weather forecast and make the programme more specific (always
     have a plan B).
12. Brief the coaching team, sailors and parents.
13. Run the weekend- make it specific to the conditions (keep it flexible).
14. Review goals and training after each training weekend/regatta. Prioritise, focus
     and record.

3.9   Safety

As an RYA coach you are responsible for the safety of all the participants involved in your sessions. There is no room for complacency.

Risks need to be assessed and adequate safety precautions taken to minimise them. This includes good planning and carrying appropriate equipment at all times.

RISK ASSESSMENTS:
"You must take reasonable care to avoid acts or omissions which you could reasonably foresee which would be likely to injure your sailor"

Coaches have a duty of care to those they are working with – failure to do so could result in a claim for negligence.

Key planning factors
- Students' ability, gender and age.
- Weather (Forecast and conditions observed).
- Ratios of safety boats/coach boats to students.
- Types of boat sailed.
- Rescue facilities.
- Ability and training currency of assistants.
- Time available.
- Facilities and coaching kit available.

- Coaching team available.
- Insurance.
- Medical conditions of the students/coach/assistants.
- Communications (coach to sailor, coach to assistants, coach to shore).
- Emergency routines.
- Other club activities.
- Hazards associated with sailing at that club.
- Tide and tidal flow.
- Training goals and programme.

Coaching operating essentials:
- Medical information form.
- Parental consent forms (if under 18).
- Insurance: club, coaching, rib, dinghy.
- Child protection procedures.
- Risk assessments.
- Personal first aid certificate (6 hrs including hypothermia).
- Power boat level 2 qualification.

Top tips for risk assessments:
- What accidents are likely? How can I prevent or minimise them?
- Always ask, What if……?
- Make it part of your daily routine.
- Write it down when you can.
- Have I got enough resources and helpers?

Thoughts and questions to ask if it's too windy:
- What is my/their/the boats limit?
- What is the worst that could happen? Where would the boats end up if they capsized and drifted off?
- Can I get hold of more rescue boats?
- Can I vary the course to minimise capsizing/damage?
- Can I take them out in smaller groups?
- Send out an experienced sailor to test the conditions.
- Where is the most sheltered place to sail?
- What are the emergency procedures/communication (check before you go afloat).
- What is my non sailing alternative? Shore drills, lessons, etc (Plan B).

Loco parentis

When dealing with sailors or assistants under 18 you need to take the precautions a reasonable parent would take to look after their child:

Children below the age of 11 - Inexperienced sailors: Duty of care is at its highest. Constant supervision needed. Particular care must be shown in not exposing a child to danger - afloat, ashore, or at the water's edge.

Children below the age of 11 - Experienced sailors: Same principles as above, except children may be expected to cope with more difficult weather. But it is unlikely to be acceptable to claim that the child willingly accepted the risk.

Children 11-13 - Inexperienced sailors: The same principles as for younger children while afloat, although a lower level of supervision would be expected while ashore or at the water's edge.

Children 11-13 - Experienced sailors: Variations in children having sufficient maturity to make decisions about risk taking. While a degree of supervision is still expected, they can be reasonably expected to be self-reliant afloat and ashore. However, some may under-estimate the risks, or take risks due to peer pressure.

Young people 14-18 - Inexperienced sailors: The same principles as for younger sailors while afloat, although a very much lower level of supervision would be expected ashore or at the water's edge.

Young people 14-18 - Experienced sailors: Depending on mental maturity, can be expected to make sensible decisions about exposure to risk. By 16 or so they would be equated by the courts to adults. But the age of legal majority is 18, so any contractual documents, including exclusion of liability clauses, would probably be of no effect in law and should not be relied upon.

3.10   Child protection

Good practice protects everyone – children, volunteers and staff.

All RYA Coaches working with sailors under 18 must have read and understood the Child Protection Policy, detailed at www.rya.org.uk. If you are unable to access the website call Racing Division for a copy.

Good practice:
- Avoid spending any significant time working with children in isolation.
- Do not take children alone in a car, however short the journey.
- Do not take children to your home as part of your organisation's activity.
- Where any of these are unavoidable, ensure that they only occur with the full knowledge and consent of someone in charge of the organisation or the child's parents.
- Design training programmes within the ability of the individual child.
- If a child is having difficulty with a wetsuit or buoyancy aid, ask them to ask a friend to help if at all possible.
- If you do have to help a child, make sure that you are in full view of others, preferably another adult.

You should never:
- Engage in rough, physical or sexually provocative games.
- Allow or engage in inappropriate touching of any form.
- Allow children to use inappropriate language unchallenged, or use such language yourself when with children.
- Make sexually suggestive comments to a child, even in fun.
- Fail to respond to an allegation made by a child; always act.
- Do things of a personal nature that children can do for themselves.

It may sometimes be necessary to do things of a personal nature for children, particularly the very young or disabled. These tasks should only be carried out with the full understanding and consent of the child (where possible) and their parents/ carers. In an emergency which requires this type of help, parents should be fully informed. Be sensitive to the child and use the utmost discretion.

Changing rooms and showers
It is preferable for adults to stay away while children are there, but bullying etc can be an issue here, and a balance should be struck. In general it is better if one adult is not alone. Extra vigilance may be required if there is public access. If it is essential, in an emergency, for a male to enter a female changing area or vice versa, it is advised they are accompanied by another adult of the opposite gender.

Handling concerns, reports or allegations about child abuse
If you are concerned about a child it is NOT your responsibility to investigate further BUT it is your responsibility to report your concerns.

Handling an allegation from a child
Always:
- Stay calm.
- Show the child you are taking what they say seriously.
- Reassure the child and stress that he/she is not to blame.
- Be careful about physical contact, it may not be what the child wants.
- Be honest; explain you have to tell someone else to be able to help.
- Make a record of what the child has said as soon as possible after the event.

Never:
- Rush into actions that may be inappropriate.
- Make promises you cannot keep (eg. you won't tell anyone).
- Ask more questions than are necessary.
- Take sole responsibility – consult someone else (ideally the designated Child Protection/Welfare Officer or the person in charge or someone you can trust).

If you suspect a child may have been the subject of any form of physical, emotional or sexual abuse or neglect, keep a record of anything the child tells you or that you have observed so it can be passed on to the statutory authorities. All information must be treated as confidential, stored securely and only shared with those who need to know.

Contact the RYA's Child Protection Co-ordinator on 02380 604104 or the NSPCC free 24 hour helpline on 0808 800 5000.

Photography and video
It is important to minimise the risk of anyone using images of children in an inappropriate way. There are two key principles:
- Before taking photos or video, obtain written consent from the child and their parents/carers for their images to be taken and used.
- When publishing images, make sure they are appropriate and that you do not include any information that might enable someone to contact the child.

3.11   Rib usage

Before use
Check there is sufficient oil (2 strokes). Fuel line is connected through filter on transom.

Important - Use only **TCW-3** rated oil (2 stroke engines). Lower rated oil will invalidate the engine warranty!

Launching:
- Remove over bars where clearance between boat and bars is in doubt.
- Remove lighting board and fully retract bars.
- Always keep wheel bearings and axle clear of water (both launching and recovering). Continuous submerging will lead to seized bearings.
- Always keep bow winch strap attached until ready to launch.
- Never rely solely on the handbrake to stop trailer.
- Once launched keep all covers, over bars, ties and light board together with trailer.
- Clamp trailer.
- Avoid leaving handbrake on for anything over short periods as this can lead to seizing brakes. Clamp and chocks should be used to anchor trailer.

Once afloat:
- Never start engine with prop clear of the water.
- Once started check that there is a cooling jet from back of engine, if not do not use (report).
- Always use the kill cord.
- Allow engine to warm up before using high revs (3 minutes min).

- Use extreme caution when unsure of water depth and use tilt to avoid grounding.
- Avoid over tilting and exposing cooling intake.
- Avoid grounding hull.
- Do not place heavy objects on control cables.
- Do not moor up against pontoons and quays in exposed conditions or where likely to cause wear or damage.
- For safety, always use an additional painter when mooring overnight.

Recovering:
- Ensure you have help shore side and they are briefed.
- Person/s in wet gear will be preferable to help guide boat onto trailer (using sailors in sailing kit a good idea).
- Set up trailer on slipway with bearings/brakes etc. clear of water.
- Pull through winch strap ready to attach.
- Approach trailer slowly and with sufficient engine tilt to avoid the prop grounding.
- Ensure any helpers are clear of rear of trailer but ready to guide bow onto rollers.
- When strap is attached begin winching on, fully tilt engine and make any final alignment adjustments.
- Dress boat - strapping/securing at the stern and bow. To avoid engine dropping down apply tilt support lever.

Caution – do not rely on winch strap to secure RIB when on steep incline, use painter as 'safety' to secure RIB before pulling boat to flat ground.

Basic trouble shooting

Trailer brakes seized/wheels locked up:
- Try towing forward then back several times.
- Use something solid to tap brake drum on inside of trailer wheel.

Engine suddenly runs roughly or alarm sounds:
- 2 Stroke Engines - Turn engine off, lift off cover, check oil level and fill if required (usually occurs when the oil level reads under half full).

Engine fails to start:
- Check kill cord attached.
- Check fuel line attached properly.
- Check fuel level.
- Check breather screw/vent on external tanks is wound off and fuel line pump has pressure.
- Check throttle in neutral.

3.12   Coaching kids

Fun, fun, fun!
- Keep exercises short and varied.
- Don't expect children to remember long lists of instructions. Expect to explain each exercise as you reach it.
- Try carrying a stock of sweets - when they come to collect these you can give out further plans and advice.

Talking the talk:
- Communication between adults and children is a black art – don't try to sound groovy for the sake of it!
- Use names – get them to write their names on their transoms or back of their buoyancy aids.

Briefings:
- Always better in small groups to reduce distraction from within the group.
- Use video and projector to show selected clips.

The call of nature:
- Keep sessions afloat fairly short - children need to fuel up on drinks and food much more often than adults and may not always remember.
- Many are also very shy about bodily functions. For longer sessions afloat organise toileting facilities - a mother ship or fast RIB ashore.
- Beware hypothermia – it strikes quickly in a sailor with a small body-mass.

Top tips:
- Keep sessions short, and change exercises frequently.
- Use digital video, but edit the film before de-briefs.
- Do not show any favouritism.
- Make sure that all the sailors feel comfortable and safe.
- Encourage competition but don't put off those at the back – for example, with training races publish the top 10 and credit the rest with 11 – they know where they finished.
- Youngsters enjoy one-to-ones with their coach. Work on the sailor-coach relationship. Have an individual chat with each sailor every time.
- E-mail to emphasise points from a weekend and send out training notes. NB **Emails must only be sent to parents with the children copied in.**
- Few under-14s are interested in physical training. Emphasise that in heavy weather the fittest do best in the last race. Eventually the lesson sinks in.
- Carry a large bag of toffees!

3.13   Working with parents

Working with parents:
- Make sure parents know what is going on.
- Don't see parents as a threat, use them as a resource.
- Parents are usually anxious, have a meeting with them to outline how the event will be managed.
- Sometimes parents have good ideas; don't be afraid of using them.
- Don't be afraid to set standards for parents and sailors. Include what you will do if they break the rules. Yellow card, red card, sin bin!
- With younger sailors ask parents if they want to assist with logistical matters such as: water, food, boat washing, notice boards, carrying bags, shopping.
- Try to identify the parents' and sailors' expectations for what they want from the weekend.
- Getting feedback from parents can be really useful but make sure you pick someone who isn't going to be emotionally involved with their kids, has a good knowledge of sailing and knows what good coaching is about.

Establishing the parents' and coach's role:
- How to optimise the coach's time with the sailors.
- Identify key jobs/roles and write down the details. These can be sent to parents to assist them. They may never have been a helper.
- Potential roles:
  - House parent
  - Beach master
  - Launching ribs
  - Liaising with the club
  - Safety manager (deals with safety crews and runs safety brief)
- Try to create a detailed weekend plan with times and designated parents. It will save you time chasing people and make it easier to brief.

What do you need from the parents?

- Optimise the coaching time with the sailors.
- Supportive of coach and sailor (value the coach).
- Willing to pitch in and help.
- Happy to distance themselves, not get too involved.
- Consistent in their approach.
- Not to get too emotional.
- Happy to get on with the task (autonomy).
- Don't coach or pressurise the kids.
- Spend money when they have to (the right equipment).
- Prepared to listen.
- Time away from the team (personal time and space) - identify with the sailors and parents when you have 'off' time - create routines.
- Don't talk shop all of the time.

How to contact the RYA Coaching Development Team:

Coaching Development Manager
David Mellor
david.mellor@rya.org.uk
02380 604 165

Coaching Development Officer
Mike Hart
mike.hart@rya.org.uk
07720 430 902

Coaching Development & Keelboat Racing Co-ordinator
Jessica Beecher
jessica.beecher@rya.org.uk
02380 604 167

Coaching Administrator
Caroline Sullivan
caroline.sullivan@rya.org.uk
02380 604 235